UNION WITH CHRIST:
Last Adam and
Seed of Abraham

A. Blake White

Alex,
Hope this book
makes you cherish
Christ's centrality
all the more.

in Him,

Books By
A. Blake White

∞

Abide in Him
Galatians: A Theological Interpretation
The Law of Christ: A Theological Proposal
The Newness of the New Covenant

UNION WITH CHRIST:
Last Adam and
Seed of Abraham

A. Blake White

5317 Wye Creek Drive, Frederick, MD 21703-6938
301-473-8781 | info@newcovenantmedia.com
www.NewCovenantMedia.com

Union with Christ:
Last Adam and Seed of Abraham

Copyright 2012 © by A. Blake White

Cover design by Matthew Tolbert

Published by: New Covenant Media
                    5317 Wye Creek Drive
                    Frederick, Maryland 21703-6938

Orders: www.newcovenantmedia.com

Cover design by: Matthew Tolbert—www.mrtolbert.com

Printed in the United States of America

ISBN 13: 978-1-928965-42-8

To My Parents,

Jamie White

and

Randy and Lisa White

Thank you for *everything.* Much love!

Table of Contents

TABLE OF CONTENTS	IX
CHAPTER 1:	1
Introduction	
CHAPTER 2:	7
The Centrality of Union with Christ	
CHAPTER 3:	13
The Instrument of Union with Christ	
CHAPTER 4:	21
Union with the Last Adam: Image	
CHAPTER 5:	27
Union with the Last Adam: Head	
CHAPTER 6:	37
Union with the Last Adam: King	
CHAPTER 7:	41
Union with the Last Adam: Priest	
CHAPTER 8:	47
Union with the Seed of Abraham	
CHAPTER 9:	51
Union with the Seed of Abraham: Land	
CHAPTER 10:	55
Union with the Seed of Abraham: Offspring	
CHAPTER 11:	63
Union with the Seed of Abraham: Blessing	
CHAPTER 12:	67
Conclusion	
SELECT BIBLIOGRAPHY	69

Chapter 1:

Introduction

I often sign my letters with, "In Christ, Blake." I have done this since I first became a Christian, but only later did I come to realize just how significant these two words are. They mean everything! To be a Christian is to be *in Christ.* This is why Paul could say in 2 Corinthians 12:2 that he knew a man "in Christ." He could have said, "I know a Christian." In Romans 16:7, Paul says that Andronicus and Junia were "in Christ" before he was. In other words, they were Christians before he was.[1] Christians are those who are "in the Messiah."

Evangelical Christians claim to be "Christ-centered." This is good and right, for the New Testament is Christ-centered. Unfortunately, the biblical teaching on union with Christ is somewhat of a neglected theme.[2] Can you name one book dedicated to this precious truth? Odds are you can't. A couple of years ago, I would not have been able to either.

---

[1] Sinclair B. Ferguson, *The Holy Spirit* (Downers Grove, IL: IVP, 1996), 108.

[2] James D.G. Dunn, *The Theology of Paul the Apostle* (Grand Rapids: Eerdmans, 1998), 397.

Thankfully, this is changing.[3] It is unfortunate that this theme is neglected because of its pervasiveness in Scripture (as we will see). But it is also unfortunate because of the Christ-centeredness of this theme. It is all about HIM! He is the center.[4]

Union with Christ seems to be a distinctively Calvinist doctrine. That is not at all to say that other traditions do not believe in union with Christ. It is simply to say that the Calvinist tradition has given more attention to this teaching than others. Swiss theologian Emil Brunner observed in 1935 that the doctrine of union with Christ is the "center of all Calvinistic thinking."[5] That may be a bit overstated, but I hope that it increasingly becomes accurate. This is due to the central role this teaching has in John Calvin's sermons and theology.[6] At the end of the day though, I am less concerned about a tradition than I am about exegesis. Let's get biblical.

---

[3] I have heard that both Robert Letham and Kevin DeYoung are working on books on this theme. Keep an eye out for these!

[4] Traditional discussions of the *ordo salutis* (order of salvation) can be counterproductive in this regard. One can go on discussing calling, regeneration, justification, sanctification, and glorification, and Christ is left out of the discussion. If not displacing him, he is certainly sidelined.

[5] Emil Brunner, *Vom Werk des heiligen Geist* (Tubingen, 1935), 38, quoted in Lewis B. Smedes, *Union with Christ* (Grand Rapids: Eerdmans, 1983), 31.

[6] See Mark A. Garcia, *Life in Christ: Union with Christ and Two-fold Grace in Calvin's Theology* (Eugene, OR: Wipf and Stock, 2008); William B. Evans, *Imputation and Impartation: Union with Christ in American Reformed Theology* (Eugene, OR: Wipf and Stock, 2009).

Union with Christ is a distinctly Pauline teaching.[7] He, in particular, uses the phrase "in Christ" (*en Christō*) all the time. The phrase occurs numerous times and can have different shades of meaning depending on the context. The expressions "in Christ," "in the Lord," "in Christ Jesus," "in him," etc., occur 164 times in Paul's writings and 26 times in John's writings.[8] As New Testament scholar Mark Seifrid writes, "The variety of ways in which the phrases appear in Paul's letters indicates that they serve as a flexible idiom which may express instrumentality or mode of action as well as locality. ...In varying ways, then, the expression 'in Christ' conveys Paul's belief that God's saving purposes are decisively effected through Christ."[9]

It is best to take the "in" (*en*) in "in Christ" in a locative sense, describing the believer's new situation, sphere, or environment. We have been transferred out of darkness into

---

[7] Lewis B. Smedes, *Union with Christ* (Grand Rapids: Eerdmans, 1970), xi.

[8] Hoekema, *Saved By Grace*, 65; Stewart, *A Man in Christ*, 155; William A. Mueller, "The Mystical Union," in *Basic Christian Doctrines*, ed. Carl F.H. Henry (New York: Holt, Rinehart, and Winston, 1962), 208; R.E.O. White, *Biblical Ethics* (Atlanta: John Knox, 1979), 151; Smedes, *Union with Christ*, 55; Demarest says the cognate expressions of "in Christ" occurs 216 times in the Pauline literature in *The Cross and Salvation*, (Wheaton, IL: Crossway, 1997), 313; Keathley also notes that Paul uses such expressions 216 times as well in "The Work of God: Salvation," 688.

[9] Mark A. Seifrid, "In Christ," in *Dictionary of Paul and His Letters*, ed. Hawthorne, Gerald F., Ralph P. Martin, and Daniel G. Reid (Downers Grove, IL: IVP, 1993), 433.

marvelous light. We have been transferred from the realm of Adam into the realm of Christ. We are no longer occupied in the "flesh territory" but have been transferred into "Spirit territory." We have been rescued from the era of law and ushered into the era of grace (Rom 6:14). Being in Christ marks the end of the old existence and the beginning of the new.[10]

Scripture can speak of us being in Christ (2 Cor 5:17; John 15:4, 5, 7; 1 Cor 15:22; 2 Cor 12:2; Gal 3:28; Eph 1:4; Phil 3:9; 1 Thess 4:16; 1 John 4:13) and of Christ being in us (Gal 2:20; Col 1:27; Rom 8:10; 2 Cor 13:5; John 17:21, 14:20; Eph 3:17). Some passages teach both in the same passage. Consider the following three verses from John's writing:

> John 6:56 - *Whoever feeds on my flesh and drinks my blood abides in me, and I in him.*

> John 15:4 - *Abide in me, and I in you.*

> 1 John 4:13 - *By this we know that we abide in him and he in us, because he has given us of his Spirit.*

As Reformed theologian Anthony Hoekema puts it, "It would seem, therefore, that these two types of expression are interchangeable. When we are in Christ, Christ is also in us. Our living in him and his living in us are inseparable as finger and thumb."[11]

So how shall we define the doctrine of union with Christ? Systematic theologian Wayne Grudem writes, "Union with

---

[10] Bruce Longenecker, *The Triumph of Abraham's God* (Nashville: Abingdon Press, 1998), 65; Demarest, *The Cross and Salvation*, 323.

[11] Anthony A. Hoekema, *Saved By Grace* (Grand Rapids: Eerdmans, 1989), 55.

Christ is a phrase used to summarize several different relationships between believers and Christ, through which Christians receive every benefit of salvation. These relationships include the fact that we are in Christ, Christ is in us, we are like Christ, and we are with Christ."[12] Southern Baptist theologian Kenneth Keathley defines union with Christ as "an all-encompassing phrase that presents the two aspects of salvation—the positional component and the experiential component—encapsulating all the benefits believers receive from Jesus Christ."[13] These definitions are appropriately comprehensive. It has to be to do justice to all the varied biblical data.

It is also important to point out that we are united to Christ individually and corporately. We Americans have a bad habit of reading the New Testament as if it were addressed to us as individuals rather than to congregations. What is true of the individual is also true of the community. It is doubtful Paul separated these concepts in his thinking.[14] We shouldn't separate them either.

---

[12] Wayne Grudem, *Systematic Theology* (Grand Rapids: Zondervan, 1994), 840.

[13] Kenneth Keathley, "The Work of God: Salvation," in *A Theology for the Church*, ed. Daniel L. Akin (Nashville: B&H Academic, 2007), 692.

[14] Bruce Demarest, *The Cross and Salvation,* 327, 331.

Chapter 2:

The Centrality of Union with Christ

Union with Christ is central to the doctrine of salvation.[15] Calvin, in the first paragraph of Book Three of *The Institutes*, says, "First, we must understand that as long as Christ remains outside of us, and we are separated from him, all that he has suffered and done for the salvation of the human race remains useless and of no value for us."[16] We receive no blessing of the gospel outside of our union with Christ. We

---

[15] Sinclair Ferguson calls it the foundation of the Christian life in *The Christian Life* (Carlisle, PA, 2005), 104; Scot McKnight believes union with Christ is foundational to all atonement theories, *A Community Called Atonement* (Nashville: Abingdon Press, 2007), 109-10; Richard B. Gaffin says it is a most basic element in Paul's soteriology and apart from it the structure of the whole cannot be grasped in *Resurrection and Redemption* (Phillipsburg, NJ: P&R Publishing, 1978), 59; idem., *By Faith Not By Sight,* where he writes, "To sum up: present union with Christ – sharing with him in all he has accomplished and now is by virtue of his death and resurrection – that, as much as anything, is at the center of Paul's soteriology;" Robert Letham, *The Work of Christ,* 75, 80, 81, 86, 184, 189; It is strange that J.I. Packer does not include a chapter on union with Christ in his *Concise Theology* (Wheaton, IL: Tyndale, 1993).

[16] John Calvin, *Institutes of the Christian Religion Vol. 1,* trans. Ford Lewis Battles, ed. John T. McNeill (Louisville: Westminster John Knox Press, 2006), 3.1.1, 537.

have been blessed with *every spiritual blessing* in Christ (Eph 1:3). All of God's goodness is mediated to us in union with the Messiah, our representative.[17] Since all the blessings of salvation are found *in Christ*, union with Christ is the central blessing of the gospel.[18]

One of the most important works with this reality in mind is John Murray's *Redemption Accomplished and Applied*. In it, he writes that union with Christ "underlies every step of the application of redemption. Union with Christ is really the central truth of the whole doctrine of salvation not only in its application but also in its once-for-all accomplishment in the finished work of Christ."[19] In 1 Corinthians 1:30-31, Paul writes, "It is because of him that you are in Christ Jesus, who has become for us wisdom from God—that is, our right-eousness, holiness and redemption. Therefore, as it is writ-ten: 'Let the one who boasts boast in the Lord.'" In Christ we are regenerated, justified, sanctified, adopted, and redeemed from the power of Satan.[20]

Consider how many times Paul alludes to union with Christ in Ephesians 1:3-13 (my emphasis):

---

[17] Demarest, *The Cross and Salvation*, 336.

[18] Graham A. Cole, *He Who Gives Life* (Wheaton, IL: Crossway, 2007), 240; Sinclair Ferguson, *The Holy Spirit*, 102.

[19] John Murray, *Redemption Accomplished and Applied* (Grand Rapids: Eerdmans, 1955), 161; Similarly, Kenneth Keathley writes, "Union with Christ is not one phase or aspect of salvation; it is the whole of salvation in which all other aspects are subsets," "The Work of God: Salvation," 687.

[20] Robert Letham, *The Work of Christ* (Downers Grove, IL: IVP, 1993), 184.

*Praise be to the God and Father of our Lord Jesus Christ, who has blessed us in the heavenly realms with every spiritual **blessing in Christ**. (1:3)*

*For he chose us **in him** before the creation of the world to be holy and blameless in his sight. (1:4)*

*In love he predestined us for adoption to sonship **through Jesus Christ**, in accordance with his pleasure and will (1:5)*

*To the praise of his glorious grace, which he has freely given us **in the One** he loves. (1:6)*

***In him** we have redemption through his blood, the forgiveness of sins, in accordance with the riches of God's grace (1:7)*

*He made known to us the mystery of his will according to his good pleasure, which he purposed **in Christ**, (1:9)*

*To be put into effect when the times reach their fulfillment — to bring unity to all things in heaven and on earth **under Christ**. [Literally en tō Christō] (1:10)*

***In him** we were also chosen, having been predestined according to the plan of him who works out everything in conformity with the purpose of his will, (1:11)*

*In order that we, who were the first to put our hope **in Christ**, might be for the praise of his glory. (1:12)*

*And you also were included **in Christ** when you heard the message of truth, the gospel of your salvation. When you believed, you were marked **in him** with a seal, the promised Holy Spirit, (1:13)*

It is clear from this packed paragraph that union with Christ was at "the heart of Paul's religion."[21]

---

[21] Stewart, *A Man in Christ,* 147. Stewart writes that union with Christ is the key that unlocks the secrets of Paul's soul.

Consider the same theme in Colossians:

To God's holy people in Colossae, the faithful brothers and sisters **in Christ:** *(1:2)*

In whom *we have redemption (1:14)*

For **in him** *all things were created (1:16)*

For God was pleased to have all his fullness dwell **in him** *(1:19)*

But now he has reconciled you **by [en] Christ's** *physical body through death to present you holy in his sight (1:22)*

To them God has chosen to make known among the Gentiles the glorious riches of this mystery, which is **Christ in you,** *the hope of glory. (1:27)*

In whom *are hidden all the treasures of wisdom and knowledge. (2:3)*

So then, just as you received Christ Jesus as Lord, continue to live your lives **in him,** *(2:6)*

Rooted and built up **in him** *(2:7)*

For **in Christ** *all the fullness of the Deity lives in bodily form, (2:9)*

And **in Christ** *you have been brought to fullness. He is the head over every power and authority. (2:10)*

In him *you were also circumcised with a circumcision not performed by human hands. (2:11)*

Having been buried **with him** *in baptism, in which you were also raised* **with him** *through faith in the working of God, who raised him from the dead. (2:12)*

God made you alive **with Christ.** *(2:13)*

He made a public spectacle of them, triumphing over them **by the** *cross.* [I think the NIV is correct with "by the cross" (literally "in or by it") here, but it could be translated *"in him" (en autō)*—so the ESV]

Since you died **with Christ** *to the elemental spiritual forces of this world (2:20)*

Since, then, you have been raised **with Christ**, *set your hearts on things above (3:1)*

For you died, and your life is now hidden **with Christ** *in God. (3:3)*

Children, obey your parents in everything, for this pleases the Lord. [Literally *"For this is pleasing* **in the Lord**" *(en kuriō)*—so the NET].

He is a dear brother, a faithful minister and fellow servant **in the Lord.** *(4:7)*

See to it that you complete the ministry you have received **in the Lord.** *(4:17)*

These observations make it hard to disagree with James S. Stewart, who writes, "The conviction has grown steadily upon me that union with Christ, rather than justification or election or eschatology, or indeed any of the other great apostolic themes, is the real clue to an understanding of Paul's thought and experience."[22] Richard Gaffin similarly writes,

---

[22] James S. Stewart, *A Man in Christ* (Vancouver: Regent College Publishing, 1935), vii; Gaffin similarly writes, "Not justification by faith but union with the resurrected Christ by faith (of which union, to be sure, the justifying aspect stands out perhaps most prominently) is the central motif of Paul's applied soteriology," *Resurrection and Redemption,* 132; Reformed theologian Robert Reymond calls union with Christ an all-embracive relationship and the fountainhead from which flows the Christian's every spiritual blessing," *A New Systematic Theology of the Christian Faith* (Nashville: Thomas Nelson Publishers, 1998), 736, 739.

"The central soteriological reality is union with the exalted Christ by Spirit-created faith."[23]

Union with Christ is comprehensive; it is broad and embracive.[24] It extends from eternity to eternity.[25] As John Murray put it, "As far back as we can go in tracing salvation to its foundation we find 'union with Christ'; it is not something tacked on; it is there from the outset."[26] Our _entire_ lives as believers are exercised in relation to Christ: his life, values, power, and rule.[27] How does this reality come about?

---

[23] Richard B. Gaffin, _By Faith, Not By Sight_ (Waynesboro, GA: Paternoster Press, 2006), 43.

[24] Murray, _Redemption Accomplished and Applied,_ 161, 165; Richard B. Gaffin, "Union with Christ: Some Biblical and Theological Reflections," in _Always Reforming_, ed. A.T.B. McGowan (Downers Grove, IL: IVP Academic, 2006), 274-75.

[25] Hoekema, _Saved By Grace,_ 55; Gaffin, "Union with Christ," 272.

[26] John Murray, _Redemption Accomplished and Applied_ (Grand Rapids: Eerdmans, 1955), 162.

[27] Demarest, _The Cross and Salvation,_ 332.

Chapter 3:

The Instrument of Union with Christ

How do we become united to Christ? Is it through faith, as Luther puts it?

> The doctrine of faith must be kept pure, namely that through faith you are so closely united with Christ that you and He turn, as it were, into one person which cannot be separated from Him but constantly clings to Him, so that you can say with confidence: I am Christ, that is, Christ's righteousness, victory, life, etc., are mine; and Christ, in turn, says: I am this sinner, that is, his sins, death, etc., are Mine because he clings to Me and I to him; for through faith we have been joined together into one flesh and bone. 'We are members of His body, of His flesh, and of His bones' (Eph 5:30). So this faith couples Christ and me more closely than husband and wife are coupled.[28]

Many Reformed theologians likewise teach that believers are united to Jesus through faith.[29] If we are united to Christ through faith, what about those passages that teach that we

---

[28] Martin Luther in Edward M. Plass, *What Luther Says* (St. Louis, MO: Concordia Publishing, 1959), 498; Calvin teaches the same in the *Institutes* (see 3.3.1).

[29] Gaffin, *Resurrection and Redemption,* 44, 140, 142; idem., *By Faith, Not by Sight,* 42; Demarest, *The Cross and Salvation,* 337; Reymond, *A New Systematic Theology,* 736; Letham, *The Work of Christ,* 80, 81, 82.

are united to Christ *through baptism*? For example, Romans 6:3-4 says, "Or don't you know that all of us who were baptized into Christ Jesus were baptized into his death? We were therefore buried with him through baptism into death in order that, just as Christ was raised from the dead through the glory of the Father, we too may live a new life." Galatians 3:27 reads, "For all of you who were baptized into Christ have clothed yourselves with Christ." Colossians 2:12 reads, "Having been buried with him in baptism, in which you were also raised with him through your faith in the working of God, who raised him from the dead." When we were baptized, we were baptized *into* Christ. We were buried and raised *with him* in baptism. As Lewis Smedes puts it, "Union with Christ occurs for us at the moment of our baptism. We did not die with him back in A.D. 30 at Calvary outside Jerusalem, but rather in our own time at the baptismal font in our local church. There is no getting around Paul's plain language."[30]

Is the Roman Catholic teaching on baptism right after all? No, it is not quite that simple. As theologian Robert Letham writes, "Union with Christ exists in faith but it is also connected in the New Testament with baptism."[31] Dr. Letham goes on to state that baptism and faith are integrally related. He even goes so far as to say that "Baptism requires faith."[32] Now, as a Baptist I say "amen" to that! Dr. Letham is a Presbyterian though, so I am not sure how his practice lines up

---

[30] Smedes, *Union with Christ*, 99.

[31] Letham, *The Work of Christ*, 81.

[32] Ibid., 82.

with this theology. Presbyterians uniquely separate faith and baptism. For the New Testament, as well as for Baptists, Catholics, and Lutherans, baptism and faith are connected.[33] Ulrich Zwingli introduced a theological novelty to the church when he separated them.[34]

There is a lot of confusion over the issue of baptism today after 2,000 years of church history, but there was no confusion in the 1st century. For them, baptism was part of what Robert Stein has called "the conversion-initiation experience" of becoming a Christian. In the 1st century, new converts were baptized immediately. For this reason, the New Testament writers can speak of baptism right alongside faith and repentance. In fact, Stein rightfully shows that repentance, baptism, and receiving the Spirit are interrelated and are all integral parts of the experience of becoming a Chris-

---

[33] See Jonathan H. Rainbow's excellent essay "Confessor Baptism: The Baptismal Doctrine of the Early Anabaptists," in *Believer's Baptism*, ed. Thomas R. Schreiner and Shawn D. Wright (Nashville: B&H Academic, 2006).

[34] Zwingli knew that what he was teaching was new: "In this matter of baptism – if I may be pardoned for saying it – I can only conclude that all the doctors have been in error from the time of the apostles. This is a serious and weighty assertion, and I make it with such reluctance that had I not been compelled to do so by contentious spirits, I would have preferred to keep silence. … At many points we all have to tread a different path from that taken either by ancient or more modern writers or by our own contemporaries," in "Of Baptism," in Zwingli and Bullinger, *Library of Christian Classics*, vol. 24, trans. G.W. Bromiley (Philadelphia: Westminster, 1953), 130.

tian.[35] He writes, "One can refer to becoming a Christian as 'the day they repented,' 'the day they believed,' 'the day they were baptized,' 'the day they confessed Christ,' and 'the day they received the Spirit,' or to use Johannine terminology 'the day they were born again.' All these are interrelated and integral components in the experience of conversion in becoming a Christian."[36]

Thomas Schreiner, commenting on Romans 6, writes, "The reference to baptism is introduced as a designation for those who are believers in Christ. Since unbaptized Christians were virtually nonexistent, to refer to those who were baptized is another way of describing those who are Christians, those who have put their faith in Christ."[37] As Victor

---

[35] Robert Stein, "Baptism in Luke-Acts," in *Believer's Baptism*, ed. Thomas R. Schreiner and Shawn D. Wright (Nashville: B&H Academic, 2006), 36, 41, 43.

[36] Stein, "Baptism," 52; So also Schreiner, who writes, "For Paul baptism, faith, reception of the Spirit, repentance, and confession of Christ are one complex of events that all occur at conversion," in *Romans,* 310; see also Moo, *Romans* (Grand Rapids: Eerdmans, 1996), 366; Moo similarly observes, "The New Testament connects our coming to Christ (being converted and initiated into the new covenant community) to faith, to repentance, to the gift of the Spirit, and to water baptism, in various combinations. Any of these, in a kind of metonymy, could be used to connote the whole experience – implying, of course, in each instance, the presence of all the others. Water baptism, then, as a critical New Testament rite intimately connected to our conversion experience, could be used as shorthand for the whole experience," *The Letters to the Colossians and to Philemon* (Grand Rapids: Eerdmans, 2008), 202.

[37] Thomas R. Schreiner, *Romans* (Grand Rapids: Baker, 1998), 306.

Furnish puts it, "To be baptized means to 'put Christ on' (Gal. 3:27). It stands for a change of dominion, from that of Adam (the reign of the law, sin, and death) to that of Christ (the reign of grace, Rom. 5:20; 6:14; cf. 5:17)."[38] "To be baptized into Christ is to be joined with the second Adam, the one who brings salvation in the new age."[39]

So, is the Reformation wrong to use "faith alone" as a slogan? I don't think so, because it fits the emphasis of the New Testament.[40] There are many more passages on faith than there are on water baptism, and as we have seen, faith and baptism belong together. For example, in Galatians 2:16, Paul says that we have believed *into* Christ Jesus (*eis Christon Iēsoun episteusamen*) that we may be justified. Also notice the parallels in Galatians 3:26-27: "So in Christ Jesus you are all children of God through faith, (27) for all of you who were baptized into Christ have clothed yourselves with Christ." The "you are all" of verse 26 is parallel to the "all of you" in verse 27. Verse 26 mentions faith while verse 27 mentions baptism. Ephesians 3:17 teaches that Christ dwells in our hearts *through faith.* New Testament scholar Michael Gorman

---

[38] Victor Paul Furnish, *Theology and Ethics in Paul* (Nashville: Abingdon, 1968), 174.

[39] Schreiner, *Romans,* 307.

[40] However, this may not be a slogan to live by since the only time the New Testament mentions the words "faith alone" is in James 2:24, which says, "You see that a person is considered righteous by what they do and not by faith alone."

writes, "For Paul, private belief and public confession of it—including baptism—go hand in hand."[41]

We should not separate faith from baptism. The two belong together. In the world of the New Testament, when a person believes, they are to be baptized. When they are baptized, they have believed. I want to close this section with a helpful analogy from Robert Stein.[42] Like being converted to the Christian faith, becoming married involves several different but related components that belong together. These normally include the saying of vows, the giving and receiving of rings, the pronouncement of marriage by the pastor, the signing of the marriage license, and the sexual consummation. Which of these components actually resulted in becoming married? The answer is that all of these are involved in becoming married. You wouldn't want to isolate any of them. They are all involved and take place together. It was not simply one of these single components that make a couple married. So it is with conversion. In becoming a Christian, a person believes, repents, confesses Jesus as Lord, receives the Spirit, and is baptized.

So we are united to Jesus in baptism, but I hope we have seen that this doesn't mean that baptism is now mechanical or overly sacramental. Paul could have easily said we are united to Christ through faith.[43] For him, the two go hand in hand.

---

[41] Gorman, *Cruciformity,* 123.

[42] Stein, "Baptism," 57-58.

[43] Of course this faith is a gift of God. It is Spirit worked. Sinclair Ferguson writes, "The central role of the Spirit is to reveal Christ and to

---

unite us to him," *The Holy Spirit,* 100. Smedes says the Holy Spirit is "the living contact between the victorious Jesus and all who are united with Him," *Union with Christ,* 26.

Chapter 4:

Union with the Last Adam: Image

Okay, we are united to Jesus. But what does this mean? How exactly is Jesus for us? We could say many things here. The Scriptures are replete with metaphors and realities to describe our rich relationship with Jesus. I am mainly focusing on two aspects in this book. First, Christ as Last Adam; then, Christ as the Seed of Abraham.

Adam was made in the image of God. Genesis 1:27 says, "So God created mankind in his own image, in the image of God he created them." God set up his image to rule over his creation. In the ancient Near East, a king or ruler would set up their image in distant parts of their kingdom to make sure all who saw it would know "who's boss." Adam and Eve (and all mankind following them) were to perform a similar function.[44] Mankind was made in the image of God in order to indicate God's rule. This God doesn't merely rule over part of a region. Mankind populates the whole earth, showing that Yahweh is king of the *cosmos*.

---

[44] T. Desmond Alexander, *From Eden to the New Jerusalem* (Nottingham: IVP, 2008), 78; G.K Beale, *The Temple and the Church's Mission* (Downers Grove, IL: IVP, 2004), 82-83: J.V Fesko, *Last Things First* (Scotland: Mentor, 2007), 48-49.

What exactly it means to be made in the image of God is complex and debated. A more holistic and comprehensive definition seems to fit all the evidence best to me. As theologian J.V. Fesko writes, "One finds the image of God primarily in man's role as God's vice-regent over the creation, and secondarily in his mental and spiritual faculties, his ability to relate to God, and ability to create like God."[45] So there are both structural and functional aspects to the image of God.[46] Old Testament scholar John Walton has shown that across the ancient world, and the Hebrew Bible, humans are made in the image of God in that they "embody his qualities and do his work. They are symbols of his presence and act on his behalf as his representatives."[47]

The notions of sonship and image are linked in Scripture. We know this from comparing Genesis 1 with Genesis 5:

> *Gen 1:26: Then God said, "Let us make mankind in our image, in our likeness, so that they may rule over the fish in the sea and the birds in the sky, over the livestock and all the wild animals, and over all the creatures that move along the ground."*

> *Gen 5:3: When Adam had lived 130 years, he had a son in his own likeness, in his own image; and he named him Seth.*

Notice that Genesis 5 records Adam having a *son* in his own *likeness* and *image*. We also know this from Luke's genealogy. There, he traces the line of Jesus all the way back to

---

[45] J.V Fesko, *Last Things First* (Scotland: Mentor, 2007), 47.

[46] Anthony A. Hoekema, *Created in God's Image* (Grand Rapids, MI: Eerdmans, 1986), 69, 73.

[47] John H. Walton, *Ancient Near Eastern Thought and the Old Testament* (Grand Rapids: Baker Academic, 2006), 212.

Adam and calls him "son of God" (Luke 3:38). The absence of sonship language in Genesis is probably due to sensitivity to the ancient near eastern context, and to avoid pagan concepts. Also, it may have been avoided to reserve the title for the true Son who has been so from eternity (John 1; Col 1:15-20).

Jesus came to repair the damage caused by the first Adam.[48] Herman Ridderbos writes, "What was lost in the first Adam is regained in the second in a much more glorious way."[49] Christ is the *supreme image* of God (2 Cor 4:4; Col 1:15), the true "human being who fully bears the divine image."[50] Mankind was made *in* the image of God while Jesus *is* the image of God. He uniquely reveals who God is. Hebrews 1:3 says, "The Son is the radiance of God's glory and the exact representation of his being." Jesus also, unlike Adam, is the faithful Son of God. Unlike Adam (Luke 3:38), Israel (Ex 4:22; Hos 11:1), and the Davidic son (2 Sam 7:14; Ps 2), Christ is the obedient Son who alone is fully faithful to his Father.

---

[48] Letham, *Work of Christ*, 76; Smedes, *Union with Christ*, 82-85.

[49] Herman Ridderbos, *Paul: An Outline of His Theology* (Grand Rapids: Eerdmans, 1975), 85. Robert Letham notes, "The disobedience of Adam enacted on a tree was remedied by Christ's obedience on the tree," *The Work of Christ*, 28.

[50] N.T Wright, *The Resurrection of the Son of God* (Minneapolis: Fortress, 2003), 334.

Many passages explicitly or implicitly compare the first and last Adams. Philippians 2:5-8 is one such passage. It says:

"In your relationships with one another, have the same mindset as Christ Jesus: who, being in very nature God, did not consider equality with God something to be used to his own advantage; rather, he made himself nothing by taking the very nature of a servant, being made in human likeness. And being found in appearance as a man, he humbled himself by becoming obedient to death—even death on a cross!"

Many scholars have seen a contrast between Adam and Christ in this rich passage. Christ did not consider equality with God something to be used to his own advantage. Adam grasped at equality with God in Genesis 3 so he could be like God. As Morna Hooker writes, "Adam, created in the form and likeness of God, misunderstood his position, and thought that the divine likeness was something which he needed to grasp; his tragedy was that in seizing it, he lost it. Christ, the true Adam, understood that this likeness was already his, by virtue of his relationship with God. Nevertheless [he made himself powerless]."[51]

The phrase "in the form of God" (NRSV) (*en morphe theou*) in 2:6a echoes "in the image of God" in Genesis 1.[52] The phrase "did not consider equality with God something to be

---

[51] Morna D. Hooker, *From Adam to Christ* (Eugene, Oregon: Wiph & Stock, 1990), 98.

[52] Ridderbos, *Paul,* 72-74. Also see C.K. Barrett, *From First Adam To Last* (London: Adam and Charles Black, 1962), 69ff; Peter T. O'Brien, *The Epistle to the Philippians* (Grand Rapids: Eerdmans, 1991), 263-68.

used to his own advantage" in Philippians 2:6b hearkens back to Genesis 3:5 (you will be like God) and the temptation of the first image-bearers. While the first Adam attempted to grasp equality with God, the last Adam did not use his equality with God for his own advantage but made himself nothing.

In Romans 1:19-25, Paul is probably drawing on the Adam narrative as well. God made himself known to Adam (1:19: "since what may be known about God is plain to them, because God has made it plain to them"). From creation onward God's attributes were clearly seen in the things which had been made so Adam was without excuse (1:20: "For since the creation of the world God's invisible qualities—his eternal power and divine nature—have been clearly seen, being understood from what has been made, so that people are without excuse"). Adam knew God but failed to honor him as God and his foolish heart was darkened (1:21: "For although they knew God, they neither glorified him as God nor gave thanks to him, but their thinking became futile and their foolish hearts were darkened"). Adam's fall was the result of his desire to be like God and the result was that he claimed to be wise, but in fact became a fool (Rom 1:21). He failed to give glory to God. He gave his allegiance to the serpent, rather than the creator (1:25: "They exchanged the truth about God for a lie, and worshiped and served created things rather than the Creator—who is forever praised. Amen").[53]

---

[53] See Hooker, _From Adam to Christ_, 77-78. She sees it very significant that Paul uses _eikōn_ in Rom 1:23 (cf Gen 1:26-27 LXX); James D.G. Dunn, _The Theology of Paul the Apostle_ (Grand Rapids: Eerdmans, 1998), 91-92.

Chapter 5:

Union with the Last Adam: Head

When we are united to Christ, it is not as if our essences are merged together.[54] No, union is primarily representative.[55] Jesus is the representative head of his people. He fully obeyed the Father on our behalf. Robert Letham writes, "His obedience, therefore, is ours. Correspondingly, we are in a relation of solidarity with him. All he did was for us. When he did it we were regarded by God as in him, and thus sharing in all that he achieved. This is a relation of legal and corporate solidarity (Rom. 5:12-21)."[56] This is fundamental Jewish messianic theology. What is true of the Messiah is true of

---

[54] Some have spoken of this union as "mystical." Depending on what one means by this, it can be unhelpful. This language is taken from Ephesians 5 where Paul speaks of the relation of Christ and the church as a mystery. Some simply mean that this union transcends complete human understanding (see Demarest, *The Cross and Salvation,* 320, 333; Gaffin, *By Faith, Not by Sight,* 38). Others take it to mean the reality of a highly personal and intimate union of the believer with the Lord. More accurate to Paul, mystical could be taken to mean what has been previously hidden but now made known (Gaffin, "Union with Christ," 273). I avoid the word altogether because it does not promote clarity.

[55] Demarest, *Cross and Salvation,* 324, 332.

[56] Robert Letham, *The Work of Christ* (Downers Grove, IL: IVP, 1993), 82.

his people.[57] What happened to him happened to those *with him.*[58]

---

[57] This is another way of speaking of imputation. Too often, Protestants have overemphasized justification to the neglect of union with Christ, but this leads to problems. Righteousness should be viewed as a subset under union with Christ. As Albert Schweitzer famously put it, "The doctrine of righteousness by faith is therefore a subsidiary crater, which has formed within the rim of the main crater – the mystical doctrine of redemption through being-in-Christ," *The Mysticism of Paul the Apostle* (London: Black, 1931), 225. Also, Protestants have not been exegetically careful enough when espousing imputation. The only way to maintain an exegetical grounding for imputation is by grounding imputation in union with Christ. E.g., George Ladd writes, "Paul never expressly states that the righteousness of Christ is imputed to believers," *A Theology of the New Testament,* 491; Mark Seifrid writes, "It is worth observing that Paul never speaks of Christ's righteousness as imputed to believers, as became standard in Protestantism," *Christ, Our Righteousness* (Downers Grove, IL: IVP, 2000), 174. There is scant evidence for imputation apart from union. Recall Calvin's strong words: "First, we must understand that as long as Christ remains outside of us, and we are separated from him, all that he has suffered and done for the salvation of the human race remains useless and of no value for us," *Institutes* 3.1.1. Without union with Christ, we do not gain his righteous status. Later Calvin writes, "We do not, therefore, contemplate him outside ourselves from afar in order that his righteousness may be imputed to us but because we put on Christ and are engrafted into his body in short, because he deigns to make us one with him. For this reason, we glory that we have fellowship of righteousness with him," *Institutes* 3.11.10. Leon Morris writes similarly, "He never says in so many words that the righteousness *of Christ* was imputed to believers, and it may fairly be doubted whether he had this in mind in his treatment of justification, although it may be held to be a corollary from his doctrine of identification of the believer with Christ," *The Apostolic Preaching of the Cross* (Grand Rapids: Eerdmans, 1965), 282. For careful handling of imputa-

Adam and Christ are "collective personalities."[59] They are both representative heads of mankind and both have a dramatic effect on those whom they represent.[60] Adam and Christ are corporate heads of two contrasting orders of existence.[61] Jesus is the "Omega man."[62] As Sinclair Ferguson writes, "To be 'in Adam' is to be united to him in such a way that all that Adam did in his representative capacity becomes mine, and determines my existence, whether through sin leading to death, or righteousness leading to life. In an

---

tion in relation to union see D.A. Carson, "The Vindication of Imputation," in *Justification* ed. M.A. Husbands and D.J. Treier (Downers Grove, IL: IVP, 2004), 46-78; Michael Bird, *The Saving Righteousness of God* (Eugene, OR: Wipf & Stock, 2007); Letham, *The Work of Christ* 179, 182; Ferguson, *The Holy Spirit,* 104-06; Gaffin, *By Faith, Not By Sight,* 51, 122-24; idem., *Resurrection and Redemption,* 123-24; Demarest, *The Cross and Salvation,* 320, 337; Scot McKnight, *A Community Called Atonement* (Nashville: Abingdon, 2007), 96-97; Brian Vickers, *Jesus' Blood and Righteousness* (Wheaton, IL: Crossway, 2006); Lane G. Tipton, "Union with Christ and Justification," in *Justified in Christ* (Great Britain: Mentor, 2007), 23-50.

[58] This is how Paul can say that we died with Christ, we were buried with Christ, and we were raised with Christ (Col 3; Rom 6; Eph 2).

[59] Witherington, *Paul's Narrative Thought World* (Louisville: Westminster John Knox, 1994), 142.

[60] Ibid.

[61] L.J Kreitzer, "Adam and Christ," in *Dictionary of Paul and His Letters*, ed. Gerald F. Hawthorne, Ralph P. Martin, Daniel G. Reid (Downers Grove, IL: IVP, 1993), 9-15; Smedes, *Union with Christ,* 38.

[62] Witherington, *Paul's Narrative Thought World,* 146.

analogous way, to be 'in Christ' means that all he has done for me representatively becomes mine actually."[63]

One's location determines one's eternity. The rule of real estate is also the rule of salvation: location, location, location.[64] Redemption is an act of relocation.[65] As L.J. Kreitzer puts it, "We could even summarize Paul's understanding of Christian redemption as the transition from being 'in Adam' to being 'in Christ' as the saving movement from one sphere of life, one realm of existence, to another."[66]

Christ is the beginning of the new humanity.[67] Ephesians 2:14-16 says, "For he himself is our peace, who has made the

---

[63] Ferguson, *The Holy Spirit,* 108-9.

[64] Graham A. Cole, *God the Peacemaker* (Downers Grove, IL: IVP, 2009), 160.

[65] So Graham Cole writes, "Union with Christ by the Spirit relocates the believer from Adam to Christ," *He Who Gives Life,* 240-41.

[66] Kreitzer, "Adam and Christ," 11. John B. Polhill similarly writes, "Paul conceived of salvation in terms of 'power spheres' or 'dominions.' Before Christ we lived 'in the flesh,' under the power of the present evil age (1:4), under the dominion of law, of sin, and of death. In Christ we died to the old dominion and were raised to the new existence of righteousness, of life, and of the Spirit. No longer do we live in the old humanity; we live in the new humanity in Christ, and Christ lives in us. ... To be 'in Christ' is to be incorporated into the people of the Messiah ... To be 'in Christ' is to belong to the new humanity of the 'Second Adam'. ... There is no fuller expression for the totality of the Christian life than Paul's language of incorporation into Christ," *Paul and His Letters* (Nashville: B&H Publishers, 1999), 146-47.

[67] Mark A. Seifrid, "In Christ," in *Dictionary of Paul and His Letters,* ed. Gerald F. Hawthorne, Ralph P. Martin, Daniel G. Reid (Downers Grove, IL: IVP, 1993), 435; Letham, *Work of Christ,* 79; Douglas Moo, "The Law of Christ as the Fulfillment of the Law of Moses," in *Five*

two groups one and has destroyed the barrier, the dividing wall of hostility, by setting aside in his flesh the law with its commands and regulations. His purpose was to create in himself one new humanity out of the two, thus making peace, and in one body to reconcile both of them to God through the cross, by which he put to death their hostility." Jesus is the one new man (*hena kainon anthropon*) who represents the new humanity "comprising Jews and Gentiles who have been united in Christ as the inclusive representative of the new order."[68]

Adam is the head of the old age and Jesus is the head of the new age.[69] Geerhardus Vos has said that "the comprehensive antitheses of the First Adam and the Last Adam, sin and righteousness, the flesh and the Spirit, law and faith," are "precisely the historic reflections of the one great transcendental antithesis between this world and the world-to-come."[70] The first Adam is in charge of this present evil age while the last Adam is in charge of the age to come, which has invaded the present through his rising from the dead. The age to come has begun; the new creation has dawned; eschatology has been inaugurated in Christ's resurrection

---

Views on Law and Gospel ed. Stanley N. Gundry (Grand Rapids: Zondervan, 1999), 321.

[68] Peter T. O'Brien, *The Letter to the Ephesians* (Grand Rapids: Eerdmans, 1999), 331.

[69] Smedes, *Union with Christ,* 20-25.

[70] Geerhardus Vos, *The Pauline Eschatology* (Phillipsburg, NJ: P&R Publishing, 1994), 60-61.

from the dead.[71] The Jews rightly saw that resurrection would come at the end of the age (Dan 12:2). What they did not expect was one man to be raised in the middle of history. Jesus' empty tomb is evidence that the future has invaded the present and is the guarantee that God's kingdom will be fully consummated in the future. The new creation is here through the person and work of Jesus. As the Spirit of God hovered over the waters of the old creation (Gen 1:2), so the Spirit comes on Mary and overshadows her when she conceived the Son of God, inaugurating the new creation (Luke 1:35). Commenting on Luke 1:35, Robert Letham writes, "His unique conception by the Holy Spirit set him apart as the inaugurator of a new humanity of which he, as the second Adam, was head."[72]

The clearest connection between Adam and Christ comes in Romans 5:12-19 and 1 Corinthians 15. In Romans 5, Paul writes of Adam as "a pattern [*typos*] of the one to come" (5:14). He makes a typological connection between the two. "Sin entered the world through one man. ... just as one trespass resulted in condemnation for all people, so also one righteous act resulted in justification and life for all people. For just as through the disobedience of the one man the many were made sinners, so also through the obedience of the one man the many will be made righteous" (5:12a, 18-19). Adam, as the representative head of the human race,

---

[71] Gaffin, *By Faith,* 61.

[72] Letham, *The Work of Christ,* 79. There he also writes, "The birth of Jesus thus marks a new creation, a new beginning, equally due to the creative energies of God."

acts on behalf of his people. He sinned as our representative, and we are sinners by virtue of being in corporate solidarity with him.[73] Christ, as the new representative head, acts on behalf of the new humanity, God's elect people.[74] What Adam does is determinative for those in him. What the eschatological Adam does is also determinative for those in Him.[75] Douglas Moo writes, "This 'structural' similarity between Adam's relationship to his 'descendants' and Christ's to his underlies all of vv. 15-21."[76]

---

[73] Schreiner, *Romans,* 289.

[74] It is becoming increasingly popular for some four point Calvinists to point to union with Christ to defend their position. They will say that Jesus died and made propitiation for all, but one must connect himself to Christ through faith to gain the benefits of salvation. There is one major problem with such a view: we were chosen *in Christ* before the creation of the world according to Ephesians 1:4. Union with Christ goes back before time. The elect were united to Christ in eternity, at the death and resurrection, and in their own life history at baptism/faith.

[75] Jason C. Meyer, *The End of the Law* (Nashville: B&H Academic, 2009), 54-59.

[76] Douglas Moo, *The Epistle to the Romans* (Grand Rapids: Eerdmans, 1996), 334. Similarly, Thomas Schreiner writes, "Adam and Christ are analogous in that the status of all human beings depends on the work of Adam or of Christ. The contrast between the two comes to the forefront in that Adam's impact on humanity was evil and Christ's was good. This point is so obvious that it hardly needs to be said, but the primary reason why Paul wants to emphasize the contrast between Adam and Christ is that Christ has undone and reversed the evil Adam imposed on the world. The two are not parallel in every respect, for Adam wreaked havoc on the world through his sin. The work of

Adam represents the realm of sin and death while Christ represents the realm of righteousness and life (5:20-21). Paul unpacks the fact that we have died to the power of sin by being united to Christ in baptism in Romans 6:1-14:

"What shall we say, then? Shall we go on sinning so that grace may increase? By no means! We are those who have died to sin; how can we live in it any longer? Or don't you know that all of us who were baptized into Christ Jesus were baptized into his death? We were therefore buried with him through baptism into death in order that, just as Christ was raised from the dead through the glory of the Father, we too may live a new life. For if we have been united with him in a death like his, we will certainly also be united with him in a resurrection like his. For we know that our old self was crucified with him so that the body ruled by sin might be done away with, that we should no longer be slaves to sin— because anyone who has died has been set free from sin. Now if we died with Christ, we believe that we will also live with him. For we know that since Christ was raised from the dead, he cannot die again; death no longer has mastery over him. The death he died, he died to sin once for all; but the life he lives, he lives to God. In the same way, count yourselves dead to sin but alive to God in Christ Jesus. Therefore do not let sin reign in your mortal body so that you obey its evil desires. Do not offer any part of yourself to sin as an in-

---

Christ is much more significant, for the good that he has effected also involves the undoing of the evil wrought by Adam. It is one thing to blemish what is beautiful, but is much harder to set straight what is already crooked," *Romans,* 284.

strument of wickedness, but rather offer yourselves to God as those who have been brought from death to life; and offer every part of yourself to him as an instrument of righteousness. For sin shall no longer be your master, because you are not under the law, but under grace."

At the conclusion, we would expect him to say, "For sin shall no longer be your master, because you are not under sin, but under grace." That is not what he says though. Instead he writes, "For sin shall no longer be your master, because you are not under the *law*, but under grace." This is because, for Paul, the law represents the old age, the old era of redemptive history. Law and grace here refer to different eras in God's one plan.[77] They are contrasting salvation-historical powers or realms.[78] John 1:16-17 similarly says, "Out of his fullness we have all received grace in place of grace already given. For the law was given through Moses; grace and truth came through Jesus Christ." With the Adam/Christ contrast, the law is on the side of Adam. With the old age/new age contrast, the law is on the side of the old age. Baptism brings one out of the Adam/law/sin sphere.[79] We are no longer under law but under grace. "Under grace" refers to the new age inaugurated at Christ's resurrection. Sin ruled under the old age but Christ gave himself for our sins to rescue us from the present evil age (Gal 1:4).

---

[77] Schreiner, *Romans*, 326.

[78] Moo, *Romans*, 389.

[79] N.T. Wright, "Romans," *The New Interpreter's Bible* (Nashville: Abingdon, 2002) 536.

In 1 Corinthians 15, Paul also makes an explicit Adam/Christ connection. Verses 21-22 say, "For since death came through a man, the resurrection of the dead comes also through a man. For as in Adam all die, so in Christ all will be made alive." Later, in verse 45, Christ is called "the last Adam."[80] Christ is also called the second man (v. 47). Paul's language here is insightful. Paul could have avoided using the label "second Adam" due to the fact that in many ways Noah was the second Adam. Christ is the *second* man over the second creation, and the *last* Adam. Adam represents *all* humanity, while Christ represents the *new* humanity.

So from both Romans 5 and 1 Corinthians 15 we see that Adam and Christ are corporate persons with representative acts.[81] They are representative heads of two contrasting orders of life, two ages, "two world-periods, in a word, two creations."[82] What each representative head does is "determinative, respectively, for those 'in him', as their representative."[83]

---

[80] Of verse 45, Gaffin writes, "Because of his resurrection and ascension, the incarnate Christ ('the last Adam') has been so transformed by the Spirit and is now in such complete possession of the Spirit that he has 'become life-giving Spirit,' with the result that now 'the Lord [Christ] is the Spirit'," *By Faith, Not By Sight,* 39 (cf. also 66).

[81] Kreitzer, "Adam and Christ," 12.

[82] Gaffin, *Resurrection and Redemption,* 85.

[83] Gaffin, "Union with Christ," 272.

Chapter 6:

Union with the Last Adam: King

In Genesis 1, Adam was commissioned to be the first earthly king. He was given dominion. Genesis 1:26 says, "Then God said, 'Let us make mankind in our image, in our likeness, so that they may rule over the fish in the sea and the birds in the sky, over the livestock and all the wild animals, and over all the creatures that move along the ground'." Psalm 8 is the first "God-breathed" commentary on the first chapter of Genesis, reflecting on the wonderful responsibility and privilege it is to be human. Psalm 8 is full of royal language applied to mankind: *crowned* with *glory* and *honor*, made mankind *rulers* over the works of his hands, put everything *under* their feet. Hebrews 2:5-9 quotes Psalm 8 and applies it to Jesus, the truly human one:

"It is not to angels that he has subjected the world to come, about which we are speaking. But there is a place where someone has testified: 'What is mankind that you are mindful of them, a son of man that you care for him? You made them a little lower than the angels; you crowned them with glory and honor and put everything under their feet.' In putting everything under them, God left nothing that is not subject to them. Yet at present we do not see everything subject to them. But we do see Jesus, who was made lower than the angels for a little while, now crowned with glory and honor because he suffered death, so that by the grace of God he might taste death for everyone."

David VanDrunen writes, "Jesus, as a true human being, fulfills the destiny of the human race in the original creation, namely, the destiny of enjoying dominion over the world to come with all glory and honor."[84]

New Testament scholar Greg Beale has made the case that when God created Adam in his image in the garden, Adam was to serve God as priest-king in the temple-sanctuary of Eden. We will deal with the priestly aspect in the next chapter. Beale writes, "The intention seems to be that Adam was to widen the boundaries of the Garden in ever increasing circles by extending the border of the Garden sanctuary into the inhospitable outer spaces. The outward expansion would include the goal of spreading the glorious presence of God."[85] Hence, Genesis 1:28 with the command to "Be fruitful and multiply and fill the earth and subdue it and have dominion" can be seen as the first 'Great Commission" that was repeatedly applied to humanity as history progressed.[86] Adam, as king, was to spread God's rule. He was commissioned to extend the boundaries of Eden until the whole created world would be full of God's glorious presence. Adam and Eve failed in their commission though, preferring instead to be self-ruling rather than ruled by God. As a result

---

[84] David VanDrunen, _BioEthics and the Christian Life_ (Wheaton, IL: Crossway, 2009), 48.

[85] G.K Beale, _The Temple and the Church's Mission: A biblical theology of the dwelling place of God_ (Downers Grove, IL: InterVarsity Press, 2004), 85.

[86] Ibid., 117.

of the tragedy in the garden, David and virtually every king after him failed to rule as God had ordained (Deut 17).

Unlike Adam before, as well as David, Solomon, and the rest of Israel's kings, Jesus is the truly faithful ruler.[87] He is the "seed" who has crushed the head of the serpent (Gen 3:15). He is the king who comes from Abraham (Gen 17:6, 16, cf. 35:11). As the lion of the tribe of Judah, it is from his hands that the scepter will not depart. The obedience of the nations shall be *his* (Gen 49:10). He is the Israelite King who embodies and fulfills Torah (Deut 17:14-20). He rules rightly and is expanding the kingdom of God by granting faith and repentance. The last Adam is truly fruitful.

---

[87] N.T. Wright writes, "God's intention all along was to rule the world through obedient humanity – but where is such an obedient humanity to be found? Only, at this time, in Jesus himself: because he has been totally obedient to the saving plan of God, he is now set in authority over the world," *Reflecting the Glory* (Oxford: The Bible Reading Fellowship, 1997), 175.

Chapter 7:

Union with the Last Adam: Priest

We have seen that Adam is to be seen as the first king. Kings in ancient Mesopotamia created and kept extravagant gardens so the role of Adam as a gardener further portrays him in royal terms.[88] He wasn't merely the first human king though; he was the first priest-king.[89] Eden was a garden-sanctuary; it was the first temple in garden-like form.[90] As Gordon Wenham observes, "The garden of Eden is not viewed by the author of Genesis simply as a piece of Meso-potamian farmland, but as an archetypal sanctuary, that is a place where God dwells and where man should worship him. Many of the features of the garden may also be found in later sanctuaries, particularly the tabernacle or Jerusalem temple. These parallels suggest that the garden itself is un-derstood as a sort of sanctuary."[91] Consider the similarities:[92]

---

[88] Peter J. Gentry, "Kingdom Through Covenant: Humanity as the Divine Image," *SBJT* 12, no. 1 (Spring 2008), 38.

[89] William J. Dumbrell, *The Search for Order* (Eugene, OR: Wiph & Stock, 1994), 24-25.

[90] Beale, *The Temple and the Church's Mission*, 80.

[91] Gordon J. Wenham, "Sanctuary Symbolism in the Garden of Eden Sto-ry," *Proceedings of the World Congress of Jewish Studies* 9 (1986), 19.

Eden and later sanctuaries were entered from the east (Gen 3:24; Exod 25:18-22, 26:31, 36:35; 1 Kin 6:23-29; 2 Chron 3:14; Ezek 40:6).

Eden and later sanctuaries were guarded by cherubim (Gen 3:24; Exod 25:18-22, 26:31, 36:35; 1 Kin 6:23-29; 2 Chron 3:14; Ezek 28:14, 16).

The lamp stand possibly symbolizes the tree of life (Gen 2:9, 3:22; Exod 25:31-36). Arboreal decorations adorned the temple.

The Hebrew verbs *abad* (to serve) and *samar* (to keep, guard) used in relation to Adam in the garden (Gen 2:15) are found in combination elsewhere only in passages that describe priestly duties in the sanctuary (Num 3:7-8, 4:23-24, 26, 8:25-26, 18:5-6; 1 Chron 23:32; Ezek 44:14).[93]

Gold and onyx are used to decorate later sanctuaries and priestly wardrobes (Exod 25:7, 11, 17, 31). These are mentioned in Genesis 2:11-12 first.

The Lord walks in Eden as he later does in the tabernacle (Gen 3:8; Lev 26:12; Deut 23:15; 2 Sam 7:6-7).

The river flowing from Eden (Gen 2:10) is similar to the river flowing from the future Jerusalem temple in Ezekiel 47:1-12.

---

[92] The following bullet points are taken from Alexander, *From Eden to the New Jerusalem*, 21-23. See the extensive bibliography there. See also T.D. Alexander, *From Paradise to the Promised Land* (Grand Rapids: Baker, 2002), 131; Fesko, *Last Things First*, 57-75; Beale, *The Temple and the Church's Mission*, 66-81.

[93] See Fesko, *Last Things First*, 71; Beale, *The Temple and the Church's Mission*, 66-67; Gentry, "Kingdom Through Covenant," 38.

"Adam was an archetypal priest," writes J.V. Fesko, "not a farmer. Scanning the horizon of redemptive history, we find further confirmation of the garden-temple thesis. At the end of redemptive history it is not a massive city-farm that descends out of the heavens, but a city-temple. If the end of redemptive history represents God's intentions from the beginning, then he planted a temple in Eden, not a farm."[94] Adam was supposed to guard the garden-temple from anything that was unclean, but instead he listens to Eve and fails to guard against the serpent.[95] Adam is replaced with the cherubim, having failed as priest by not guarding the purity of the garden-temple.

Luke's gospel is informative in this regard. It is not by accident that the temptation of Jesus in the wilderness follows the genealogy of Jesus Christ that ends with "Adam, the son of God" (Luke 3:38). Just as Adam was tempted, so was Christ. Sinclair Ferguson writes, "Here the *inclusion* of the whole of human history between Adam and Jesus suggests that the temptation and victory of the latter are to be interpreted in the light of the testing and defeat of the former with all its baneful entail."[96] This temptation was one of the first events in Jesus' ministry (Luke 3:38-4:14). Jesus rebuffed the temptations of the serpent, regaining enemy-occupied

---

[94] Fesko, *Last Things First*, 75.

[95] Alexander, *From Eden to the New Jerusalem*, 26; Fesko, *Last Things First*, 148; J. Richard Middleton, *The Liberating Image* (Grand Rapids: Brazos, 2005), 59.

[96] Sinclair B. Ferguson, *The Holy Spirit*, 49.

territory.[97] Jesus doesn't submit to the serpent. Adam had an abundance of food (Gen 2:16) but Jesus had been fasting for forty days. Adam failed while in paradise while Christ was victorious in the barren wilderness. Sinclair Ferguson writes, "The second man-Son thus undid what was done by the first man-son; he obeyed and overcame as the last Adam, and now no further representative is needed."[98] In the Eden "rerun" Jesus is faithful.

Psalm 110 is one of the few, but great passages that speaks of a person who embodies both the role of priest and king. Psalm 110:1-4 says, "The LORD says to my lord: 'Sit at my right hand until I make your enemies a footstool for your feet.' The LORD will extend your mighty scepter from Zion, saying, 'Rule in the midst of your enemies!' Your troops will be willing on your day of battle. Arrayed in holy splendor, your young men will come to you like dew from the morning's womb. The LORD has sworn and will not change his mind: 'You are a Priest forever, in the order of Melchizedek'." This future Lord of David will be a king and a priest. In the OT, these two offices had to be separated. Think about Saul's unlawful sacrifice (1 Sam 13:8-14), or Uzziah (2 Chron 26:16-21). This future ruler will be a king-priest. We saw hints of this with Adam, who was commissioned to rule and subdue the earth and work and keep the garden-temple (Num 3:7-8, 8:25-26). We also saw the merging of these offices in Isaiah's vision of Jesus in chapter 6. This one was sitting on a throne (as king) and the train of his robe filled the

---

[97] Ibid.

[98] Ibid.

temple (as priest). Jesus is the true priest-king. Unlike Adam, he guards the garden-temple from the evil one. This may be why Mary thought that Jesus was the gardener by mistake (John 20:15). Turns out, she was right. Unlike Adam, Jesus is the faithful king-priest-gardener.

Chapter 8:

Union with the Seed of Abraham

We now turn to what it means to be united to Christ, the true seed of Abraham. In many ways, Abraham, like Noah before him, is a new Adam. As N.T. Wright points out, "the narrative quietly makes the point that Abraham and his family inherit, in a measure, the role of Adam and Eve."[99] A rabbinic *midrash* on the book of Genesis records God as saying, "I will make Adam first and if he goes astray I will send Abraham to sort it out."[100]

Genesis chapter 12 is the key chapter for our purposes here. Recall the context: Genesis 3-11 was dark. Genesis 11 tells the story of the tower of Babel. Mankind tries to reverse God's plan. The creator is interested in filling the earth with his image, but the people of Babel try to avoid this by accessing heaven in their own strength. They want to make a name for themselves. Here we have the characteristic human way: pride, self-sufficiency, idolatry, materialism, and the illusion of infinite achievement. No matter how high they ascend, God must still descend to look at their work (see 11:5). What

---

[99] N.T Wright, *The Climax of the Covenant* (Minneapolis: Fortress Press, 1993), 22.

[100] *Gen. Rab.* 14:6, quoted in Michael Goheen, *A Light to the Nations* (Grand Rapids: Baker Academic, 2010), 27.

is God to do now? He confuses them and makes a name for another. He chooses an elderly moon-worshipping couple with no children to be the launch pad for new creation. Abram is summoned by the "God who gives life to the dead and calls into being things that were not" (Rom 4:17). As William Dumbrell writes, "What is being offered in these few verses is a theological blueprint for the redemptive history of the world, now set in train by the call of Abram."[101] No one can read the Abraham narrative and not believe in sovereign grace. Genesis 12 is the solution to the problem of Genesis 1-11.[102] As Chris Wright notes, "a new world, ultimately a new creation, begins in this text."[103]

Genesis 12:1-3 reads, "The Lord had said to Abram, 'Go from your country, your people and your father's household to the land I will show you. I will make you into a great nation, and I will bless you; I will make your name great, and you will be a blessing. I will bless those who bless you, and whoever curses you I will curse; and all peoples on earth will be blessed through you." It is helpful to note the structure of this passage. There are two imperatives, each followed by three promises:

---

[101] W.J Dumbrell, *Covenant and Creation* (London: Paternoster, 1984), 66.

[102] Christopher Wright writes, "The whole Bible could be portrayed as a very long answer to a very simple question: What can God do about the sin and rebellion of the human race? Genesis 12 through to Revelation 22 is God's answer to the question posed by the bleak narratives of Genesis 3-11. Or in terms of the overall argument of this book, Genesis 3-11 sets the problem that the mission of God addresses from Genesis 12 to Revelation 22," *Mission of God,* 195.

[103] Ibid., 199.

1. Go to the land I will show you
    a. I will make you into a great nation
    b. I will bless you
    c. I will make your name great
2. Be a blessing[104]
    a. I will bless those who bless you
    b. I will curse whoever curses you
    c. All peoples will be blessed through you[105]

It is hard to overestimate the importance of these promises *for everything.* Abraham and his family are first of all the recipients of blessing, and then they are the mediators of blessing.

---

[104] Our English translations often translate this phrase as "and you will be a blessing." This is a fine translation but the fact that it is an imperative is often missed. I prefer, "and you, be a blessing."

[105] Wright, *Mission of God,* 200-01.

Chapter 9:

Union with the Seed of Abraham: Land

Land is a very important theme in the Bible. The biblical narrative could be summarized as "The Journey from Creation to New Creation." God promises Abram that his offspring would inherit the land of Canaan (Gen 12:7, 13:14-17, 15:18-21, 17:8). One of the reasons it is so important is due to the fact that the Holy Land is intimately associated with the presence of God. We could trace this theme throughout the Canon: Eden – Tabernacle – Temple – Jesus – Church - New Eden.[106]

For the purposes of this book, I do not want to get too side-tracked by the thorny issue of land. I just want to say that the land promise is for all those who are united to *the* seed of Abraham. This is not to spiritualize the land promise.[107] The land promise remains physical, but contrary to

---

[106] See Alexander's excellent chapter, "From Sacred Garden to Holy City," in *From Eden to the New Jerusalem* as well as Beale's *The Temple and the Church's Mission.*

[107] e.g, See Gary M. Burge, *Jesus and the Land* (Grand Rapids: Baker Academic, 2010), which is great in its negative work, but lacking in its positive proposals. The land promise is not found in relationship to Jesus, but ultimately in the new earth.

dispensationalism, it encompasses much more than a plot of land in the Middle East. The land promise is fulfilled for those in Christ (Jew or Gentile) in the new earth.[108] "For no matter how many promises God has made, they are 'Yes' in Christ" (2 Cor 1:20). Only with the greatest difficulty can one exclude the land promise from "no matter how many promises God has made." The apostles universalized the land promise. From them we learn that the promise land was typological. Entrance into the promise land pointed ultimately to entrance into the new heaven and the new earth.[109] We learn how to interpret the land promise through Jesus and his apostles.

In Matthew 5:5, Jesus universalizes Psalm 37:11 to say, "Blessed are the meek, for they will inherit the earth." Concerning this passage, New Testament scholar Craig Blomberg writes, "The future reward echoes Psalm 37:11 but generalizes the promise of inheriting the land of Israel to include all of the earth. Christian hope does not look forward to inhabiting a particular country but to ruling with Christ over all the globe and ultimately to enjoying an entirely re-

---

[108] It is very interesting that Covenant theology and dispensationalism share a similar hermeneutic. Covenant theology fails to see the typological nature of circumcision while dispensationalism fails to see the typological nature of land. In this writer's opinion, New Covenant theology is more consistently Christocentric in its hermeneutic.

[109] D.A. Carson, *Matthew: Chapters 1 Through 12. EBC* (Grand Rapids: Zondervan, 1995), 134; Thomas Edward McComiskey, *The Covenants of Promise* (Grand Rapids: Baker, 1985), 51-55; O. Palmer Robertson, *The Israel of God* (Phillipsburg, NJ: P&R, 2000), 25-31.

created earth and heavens (Rev 20-22)."[110] Paul universalizes the promise to Abraham: "It was not through the law that Abraham and his offspring received the promise that he would be heir of the world" (Rom 4:13). He does the same thing in Ephesians 6:2-3: "Honor your father and mother—which is the first commandment with a promise—so that it may go well with you and that you may enjoy long life on the earth."[111] Jesus, the seed of Abraham, Davidic King, and last Adam, will rule over the whole earth (Gen 49:10, Ps 2:8).

---

[110] Craig L. Blomberg, *Matthew. NAC* (Nashville: Broadman, 1992), 99.

[111] Peter T. O'Brien writes, "Significantly, when Paul 'reapplies' the commandment to his Christian readers, he omits any reference to the land of Israel and 'universalizes' the promise," *The Letter to the Ephesians. PNTC* (Grand Rapids: Eerdmans, 1999), 444; so also T.D. Alexander, *From Paradise to the Promised Land* (Grand Rapids: Baker Academic, 2002), 142.

Chapter 10:

Union with the Seed of Abraham: Offspring

Genesis, and indeed the whole Bible, anticipates a royal descendant from Abraham who will play a major role in bringing God's blessing to all the nations of the earth. Genesis 3 promises a ruler who will defeat evil. Genesis 12 speaks of a seed who will have land, offspring and blessing. Genesis 17 tells us that kings will come from Abraham's offspring. Genesis 49 promises that the scepter will not depart from Judah.[112] In 2 Samuel 7:12-14, David is promised, "When your days are over and you rest with your ancestors, I will raise up your offspring to succeed you, your own flesh and blood, and I will establish his kingdom. He is the one who will build a house for my Name, and I will establish the throne of his kingdom forever. I will be his father, and he will be my son. When he does wrong, I will punish him with a rod wielded by men, with floggings inflicted by human hands." In this passage, we see the collective noun seed being used to describe a singular person. Paul picks up on this promise in Galatians 3:16: "The promises were spoken to Abraham and to his seed. Scripture does not say 'and to his

---

[112] T.D. Alexander, *From Paradise to the Promised Land*, 111.

seeds,' meaning many people, but 'and to your seed,' meaning one person, who is Christ."[113] Abraham's seed is interpreted as the son of David, the Messiah.[114]

Romans 15:8-12 says, "For I tell you that Christ has become a servant of the Jews on behalf of God's truth, so that
the promises made to the patriarchs might be confirmed
and, moreover, that the Gentiles might glorify God for his
mercy. As it is written: 'Therefore I will praise you among
the Gentiles; I will sing the praises of your name.' Again, it
says, 'Rejoice, you Gentiles, with his people.' And again,
'Praise the Lord, all you Gentiles; let all the peoples extol
him.' And again, Isaiah says, "The Root of Jesse will spring
up, one who will arise to rule over the nations; in him the
Gentiles will hope." In this passage, Paul quotes from every
portion of the Old Testament: history (2 Sam 22:50), law
(Deut 32:43), poetry (Ps 117:1) and prophecy (Isa 11:10).
What the Old Testament promised has begun to be realized
through Jesus Christ. The nations are blessed through Abraham's singular offspring, Jesus.

---

[113] T.D. Alexander writes, "If Genesis as a whole focuses on a royal line
of seed through which God will fulfill his promises to Abraham, then
Paul's interpretation of the term 'zera' as referring to Jesus Christ is in
keeping with the common NT understanding of Jesus as the Davidic
Messiah. Thus, Paul affirms that it is only through faith in Jesus
Christ, the 'seed' of Abraham, that Jews and Gentiles may now re-
ceive the blessing given to Abraham and become God's children,"
From Paradise to the Promised Land, 155.

[114] Richard B. Hays, *Echoes of Scripture in the Letters of Paul* (London: Yale
University Press, 1989), 85.

Acts 3:21-26 says, "Heaven must receive him until the time comes for God to restore everything, as he promised long ago through his holy prophets. For Moses said, 'The Lord your God will raise up for you a prophet like me from among your own people; you must listen to everything he tells you. Anyone who does not listen to him will be completely cut off from their people.' Indeed, beginning with Samuel, all the prophets who have spoken have foretold these days. And you are heirs of the prophets and of the covenant God made with your fathers. He said to Abraham, 'Through your offspring all peoples on earth will be blessed.' When God raised up his servant, he sent him first to you to bless you by turning each of you from your wicked ways."

Abraham's offspring, in other words, Israel, consists of all who find themselves in Christ. Contrary to traditional dispensationalism, we see this truth all over the New Testament:

> 1 Peter 2:9-10 - But you are a chosen people, a royal priesthood, a holy nation, God's special possession, that you may declare the praises of him who called you out of darkness into his wonderful light. Once you were not a people, but now you are the people of God; once you had not received mercy, but now you have received mercy.[115]

---

[115] Reflecting on this passage, Tom Wright writes, "He is saying in effect, you are the true Israel. You are the chosen race, the royal priesthood, the holy nation, God's own people. You are the people upon whom have devolved all the promises that God made to Israel. Again we should be careful to point out that the people to whom Peter is writing are not simply Gentile Christians. They are both Jewish and Gen-

Philippians 3:2-3 - Watch out for those dogs, those evildoers, those mutilators of the flesh. For it is we who are the circumcision, we who serve God by his Spirit, who boast in Christ Jesus, and who put no confidence in the flesh—

Galatians 3:7 - Understand, then, that those who have faith are children of Abraham.

Galatians 3:29 - If you belong to Christ, then you are Abraham's seed, and heirs according to the promise.

Galatians 4:28 - Now you, brothers and sisters, like Isaac, are children of promise.

Galatians 4:31 - Therefore, brothers and sisters, we are not children of the slave woman, but of the free woman.

Galatians 6:15-16 - Neither circumcision nor uncircumcision means anything; what counts is the new creation. Peace and mercy to all who follow this rule—to the Israel of God.

Ephesians 2:14-15 - For he himself is our peace, who has made the two groups one and has destroyed the barrier, the dividing wall of hostility, by setting aside in his flesh the law with its commands and regulations. His purpose was to create in himself one new humanity out of the two, thus making peace,

What is so important to see is that Jesus is the hermeneutical key! I think this is one of the distinctive points of New Covenant Theology. Israel does not equal the church, as Covenant Theology teaches. Israel equals Jesus and all who are in him. As Bruce Longenecker writes, "By means of their union with Christ (cf. 3:26-28), Christians are joined to the single seed of Abraham and thereby find themselves to be

---

tile Christians – a whole new community created in the Jewish Messiah, Jesus, to be God's true Israel for the sake of the world," *Reflecting the Glory* (Oxford: The Bible Reading Fellowship, 1997),85.

the collective 'descendants of Abraham'. The mechanism in this Christological argument is not simply one of similarity of characteristic (i.e., 'faith'), as in 3:6-7, but incorporation into true Abrahamic descent by means of participation with Christ."[116] All the promises of God find their yes in Christ (2 Cor 1:20). It is worth quoting Southern Baptist theologian Russell Moore at length on this point:

> For the new covenant apostles, Jew-Gentile unity is pivotal to the early church. It is about more than human relational harmony. Instead, it acknowledges that God's kingdom purposes are *in Christ.* He is the last man and the true Israel, the bearer of the Spirit. A Jewish person who clings to the tribal markings of the old covenant acts as though the eschaton has not arrived, as though one were still waiting for the promised seed. Both Jews and Gentiles must instead see their identities not in themselves or in the flesh but in Jesus Christ and in him alone. Jesus is the descendant of Abraham, the one who deserves the throne of David. He is the obedient Israel who inherits the blessings of the Mosaic covenant. He is the propitiation of God's wrath. He is the firstborn from the dead, the resurrection and the life. Those who are in Christ—whether Jew or Gentile—receive with him all the eschatological blessings that are due to him. In him, they are all, whether Jew or Gentile, sons of God—not only in terms of relationship with the Father but also in terms of promised inheritance (Rom 8:12-17). In

---

[116] Longenecker, *The Triumph of Abraham's God*, 133. N.T. Wright says, "To put it simply: the role traditionally assigned to Israel had devolved on to Jesus Christ. Paul now regarded him, not Israel, as God's true humanity," *The Climax of the Covenant* (Minneapolis: Fortress, 1993), 26.

Christ, they all—whether Jew or Gentile—are sons of Abraham, the true circumcision, the holy nation, and the household and commonwealth of God (Gal 3:23-4:7; Eph 2-3; Col 2:6-15; 3:3-11; 1 Pet 2:9-10). … Both Covenant theology and dispensationalism, however, often discuss Israel and the church without taking into account the Christocentric nature of biblical eschatology. The future restoration of Israel has *never* been promised to the unfaithful, unregenerate members of the nation (John 3:3-10; Rom 2:25-29)—only to the faithful remnant. The church is not Israel, at least not in a direct, unmediated sense. The remnant of Israel—a biological descendant of Abraham, a circumcised Jewish firstborn son who is approved of by God for his obedience to the covenant—receives *all* of the promises due to him. Israel is Jesus of Nazareth, who, as promised to Israel, is raised from the dead and marked out with the Spirit (Ezek 37:13-14; Rom 1:2-4). … Dispensationalists are right that only ethnic Jews receive the promised future restoration, but Paul makes clear that the "seed of Abraham" is singular, not plural (Gal 3:16). Only the circumcised can inherit the promised future for Israel. All believers—Jew and Greek, slave and free, male and female—are forensically Jewish firstborn sons of God (Gal 3:28). They are *in Christ* … In Christ, I inherit all the promises due to Abraham's offspring so that everything that is true of him is true of me. … The future of Israel then does belong to Gentile believers but only because they are in union with a Jewish Messiah.[117]

Interestingly (and perhaps inconsistently), Covenant theologian Vern Poythress agrees with this point. He writes, "Because Christ is an Israelite and Christians are in union

---

[117] Russell Moore, "Personal and Cosmic Eschatology," in *A Theology for the Church* (Nashville: B&H Academic, 2007), 867-68, 906-07.

with Christ, Christians partake of the benefits promised to Israel and Judah in Jeremiah. With who is the new covenant made? It is made with Israel and Judah. Hence it is made with Christians by virtue of Christ the Israelite."[118] Later he writes, "The argument is strongest if one does not bluntly and simplistically assert that the church is a straight-line continuation of Israel. Rather one proceeds by way of Christ himself as the center point of fulfillment of the promises. ... That is to say that we inherit what he inherits. We are sons of Abraham because he is (Gal 3:29)."[119] The question I have for Dr. Poythress is, "How can one maintain this position while remaining a paedobaptist?" If believers receive the promises of Israel by union with Christ, how can this apply to infants? Union with Christ occurs through baptism, and we have seen that the New Testament connects faith and baptism and infants can't exercise faith. It is Christ and *his* descendants who are blessed with Abraham, and Christ had no physical descendants. Jesus has no grandchildren. His descendants are *spiritual*.

As Christopher Wright observes, "The ingathering of the nations was the very thing Israel existed for in the purpose of God; it was the fulfillment of the bottom line of God's promise to Abraham. Since Jesus was the Messiah of Israel and since the Messiah embodied in his own person the identity and mission of Israel, then to belong to the Messiah

---

[118] Vern Poythress, *Understanding Dispensationalism* (Phillipsburg, NJ: P&R Publishing, 1987), 106.

[119] Ibid, 126-27.

through faith was to belong to Israel. And to belong to Israel was to be a true child of Abraham, no matter what a person's ethnicity is, for 'If you belong to Christ [the Messiah], then you are Abraham's seed and heirs according to the promise' (Gal 3:29)."[120] We should be as amazed about Gentiles being included as we are about having our sins forgiven.

---

[120] Christopher J.H Wright, *The Mission of God*, 194.

Chapter 11:

Union with the Seed of Abraham: Blessing

Blessing for the nations is the bottom line of God's promise to Abraham.[121] Blessing is a rich biblical concept that refers to God's characteristically generous and abundant giving of all good to his creatures.[122] It implies the reversal of sin's curse and the restoration of creation's fullness.[123] As Michael Goheen writes, "Blessing restores all the good that God had generously bestowed on the creation in the beginning (e.g., Gen 1:22, 28) and thus anticipates his subsequent redemptive work for the flourishing of human beings, in relationship with God, with one another, and with the nonhuman creation."[124] Acts 3:26 says, "When God raised up his servant, he sent him first to you to bless you by turning each of you from your wicked ways." Galatians 3:14 says part of the blessing is the gift of the Spirit: "He redeemed us in order that the blessing given to Abraham might come to the

---

[121] Ibid.

[122] Richard Bauckham, *Bible and Mission* (Grand Rapids: Baker Academic, 2003), 34.

[123] Michael W. Goheen, *A Light to the Nations* (Grand Rapids: Baker Academic, 2010), 31.

[124] Ibid.

Gentiles through Christ Jesus, so that by faith we might receive the promise of the Spirit." Romans 4:6-9 says the blessing is the gifts of forgiveness and righteousness: "David says the same thing when he speaks of the blessedness of the one to whom God credits righteousness apart from works: 'Blessed are those whose transgressions are forgiven, whose sins are covered. Blessed is the one whose sin the Lord will never count against them.' Is this blessedness only for the circumcised, or also for the uncircumcised? We have been saying that Abraham's faith was credited to him as righteousness."

Galatians 3:8 is a very helpful text explaining the blessing: "Scripture foresaw that God would justify the Gentiles by faith, and announced the gospel in advance to Abraham: 'All nations will be blessed through you'." The blessing promised to Abraham is justification. The nations are blessed through Abraham by being justified through faith in the seed of Abraham.

Those who are "in Christ" regardless of ethnicity will inherent the blessings promised to Abraham and his family. As Ben Witherington notes, "Paul was utterly convinced that in Christ all the promises of offspring, kings, everlasting covenant to Abraham come to fruition. Equally important, he believed that both Jewish and Gentile Christians were in some way 'in Christ' so that what is given to him is given to them."[125]

What is amazing about this story is that we play a part in it. God uses us to keep his promise. As Wright puts it, "The

---

[125] Witherington, _Paul's Narrative Thought World_, 47.

words of Jesus to his disciples in Matthew 28:18-20, the so-called Great Commission, could be seen as a Christological mutation of the original Abrahamic commission—'Go ... and be a blessing ... and all nations on earth will be blessed through you'."[126]

Abraham was blessed and he was the mediator of blessing. We are blessed to be a blessing. Election is not a doctrine to argue about but a doctrine that fuels mission. We are not blessed to sit around and debate about the details of how we are blessed.[127] Evangelism is growing the family of Abraham. Again, Wright observes, "We cannot speak biblically of the doctrine of election without insisting that it was never an end in itself but a means to the greater end of the ingathering of the nations. Election must be seen as missio-

---

[126] Wright, *The Mission of God,* 213.

[127] Speaking of Israel's election, Wright writes, "The election of Israel is fundamentally missional, not just soteriological. If we allow our doctrine of election to become merely a secret calculus that determines who gets saved and who does not, we have lost touch with its original biblical intention. God's calling and election of Abraham was not merely so that he should be saved and become the spiritual father of those who will finally be among the redeemed in the new creation (the elect, in another sense). It was rather, and more explicitly, that he and his people should be the instrument through whom God would gather that multinational multitude that no man or woman can number. Election is of course, in the light of the whole Bible, election unto salvation. But it is first of all election into mission," *The Mission of God,* 264 (cf. also 65, 329, 369).

logical, not merely soteriological."[128] God elects us to be the bearers of his purpose for humankind.[129]

Jesus is the true Israel and the true Adam.[130] As Graham Cole puts it, "Jesus is all that Israel should have been as God's Son and all that Adam and Israel should have been as God's sons. In other words, Jesus is the faithful Adam and the faithful Israel."[131]

In him we are truly human. In him we find life not death, righteousness not sin. In him we are blessed with the Holy Spirit and full and final forgiveness. In him we will inherit a renewed *cosmos*. In the meantime we are actors in the drama of God. We tell his story and as we do, God adds to Abraham's family, just as he promised he would: "Look up at the sky and count the stars—if indeed you can count them. Then he said to him, 'So shall your offspring be'" (Gen 15:5).

---

[128] Wright, *The Mission of God,* 369; Goheen, *A Light to the Nations,* 31.

[129] Lesslie Newbigin, *The Gospel in a Pluralist Society* (Grand Rapids: Eerdmans, 1989), 15. On 1 Pet 2:9-10, Tom Wright writes, "If you are the chosen race, you are chosen in order that you can reveal God to the world. If you are the royal priesthood, you are priests so that you can offer the praises of creation before God. If you are the holy nation, you are the ones who are set apart for God's purposes in his world If you are God's own people then you must embody God's love for the world, and proclaim his mighty acts," *Reflecting the Glory,* 85.

[130] Cole, *He Who Gives Life,* 160.

[131] Cole, *God the Peacemaker,* 108

Chapter 12:

Conclusion

I hope you have seen the centrality of Jesus Christ in all of Scripture. I hope the doctrine of union with Christ will be at the forefront of your thinking as a result of reading this book. We have looked at what it means to be united to Jesus Christ in his role as last Adam and seed of Abraham. There is much more we could say, but I hope this short book has stirred your affections for King Jesus. He is the center of the Bible and he must increasingly become the center of our lives. Lord, give us grace. May we decrease, and may he increase!

soli deo gloria

Select Bibliography

Alexander, T. Desmond. *From Eden to the New Jerusalem*. Nottingham: IVP, 2008.

_____. *From Paradise to the Promised Land*. Grand Rapids: Baker, 2002.

Bauckham, Richard. *Bible and Mission*. Grand Rapids: Baker Academic, 2003.

Beale, G.K. *The Temple and the Church's Mission*. Downers Grove, IL: IVP, 2004.

Blomberg, Craig L. *Matthew*. Nashville: Broadman, 1992.

Calvin, John. *Institutes of the Christian Religion*. Translated by Ford Lewis Battles. Louisville: Westminster John Knox Press, 2006.

Carson, D.A. *Matthew: Chapters 1 Through 12*. Grand Rapids: Zondervan, 1995.

Cole, Graham A. *God the Peacemaker*. Downers Grove, IL: IVP, 2009.

_____. *He Who Gives Life*. Wheaton, IL: Crossway, 2007.

Demarest, Bruce. *The Cross and Salvation*. Wheaton, IL: Crossway, 1997.

Dumbrell, W.J. *Covenant and Creation*. London: Paternoster, 1984.

_____. *The Search for Order*. Eugene, OR: Wiph & Stock, 1994.

Dunn, James D.G. *The Theology of Paul the Apostle*. Grand Rapids: Eerdmans, 1998.

Ferguson, Sinclair B. *The Holy Spirit*. Downers Grove, IL: IVP, 1996.

Fesko, J.V. *Last Things First*. Scotland: Mentor, 2007.

Furnish, Victor Paul. *Theology and Ethics in Paul*. Nashville: Abingdon, 1968.

Gaffin, Richard B. *By Faith, Not By Sight*. Waynesboro, GA: Paternoster Press, 2006.

_____. *Resurrection and Redemption*. Phillipsburg, NJ: P&R Publishing, 1978.

_____. "Union with Christ: Some Biblical and Theological Reflections." In *Always Reforming*, ed. A.T.B. McGowan, 271-88. Downers Grove, IL: IVP Academic, 2006.

Gentry, Peter J. "Kingdom Through Covenant: Humanity as the Divine Image." *SBJT* 12, no. 1 (Spring 2008): 16-42.

Goheen, Michael W. *A Light to the Nations*. Grand Rapids: Baker Academic, 2010.

Gorman, Michael J. *Cruciformity: Paul's Narrative Spirituality of the Cross.* Grand Rapids: Eerdmans, 2001.

Grudem, Wayne. *Systematic Theology.* Grand Rapids: Zondervan, 1994.

Hays, Richard B. *Echoes of Scripture in the Letters of Paul.* London: Yale University Press, 1989.

Hooker, Morna D. *From Adam to Christ.* Eugene, Oregon: Wiph & Stock, 1990.

Hoekema, Anthony A. *Created in God's Image.* Grand Rapids, MI: Eerdmans, 1986.

_____. *Saved By Grace.* Grand Rapids: Eerdmans, 1989.

Keathley, Kenneth. "The Work of God: Salvation." In *A Theology for the Church,* ed. Daniel L. Akin, 686-764. Nashville: B&H Academic, 2007.

Kreitzer, L.J. "Adam and Christ." In *Dictionary of Paul and His Letters,* ed. Gerald F. Hawthorne, Ralph P. Martin, Daniel G. Reid, 9. Downers Grove, IL: IVP, 1993.

Letham, Robert. *The Work of Christ.* Downers Grove, IL: IVP, 1993.

Longenecker, Bruce. *The Triumph of Abraham's God.* Nashville: Abingdon Press, 1998.

McKnight, Scot. *A Community Called Atonement.* Nashville:

Abingdon Press, 2007.

Meyer, Jason C. *The End of the Law*. Nashville: B&H Academic, 2009.

Moore, Russell D. "Personal and Cosmic Eschatology." In *A Theology for the Church*, ed. Daniel L. Akin, 686-764. Nashville: B&H Academic, 2007.

Mueller, William A. "The Mystical Union." In *Basic Christian Doctrines*, ed. Carl F.H. Henry, 206-12. New York: Holt, Rinehart, and Winston, 1962.

Murray, John. *Redemption Accomplished and Applied*. Grand Rapids: Eerdmans, 1955.

Newbigin, Lesslie. *The Gospel in a Pluralist Society*. Grand Rapids: Eerdmans, 1989.

O'Brien, Peter T. *The Letter to the Ephesians*. Grand Rapids: Eerdmans, 1999.

Plass, Edward M. *What Luther Says*. St. Louis, MO: Concordia Publishing, 1959.

Polhill, John B. *Paul and His Letters*. Nashville: B&H Publishers, 1999.

Rainbow, Jonathan H. ""Confessor Baptism": The Baptismal Doctrine of the Early Anabaptists." In *Believer's Baptism*, ed. Thomas R. Schreiner and Shawn D. Wright, 189-206. Nashville: B&H Academic, 2006.

Reymond, Robert L. *A New Systematic Theology of the Chris-*

tian Faith. Nashville: Thomas Nelson Publishers, 1998.

Ridderbos, Herman. *Paul: An Outline of His Theology.* Grand Rapids: Eerdmans, 1975.

Seifrid, Mark A. "In Christ." In *Dictionary of Paul and His Letters,* ed. Hawthorne, Gerald F., Ralph P. Martin, and Daniel G. Reid, 433-436. Downers Grove, IL: IVP, 1993.

Schreiner, Thomas R. *Romans.* Grand Rapids: Baker, 1998.

Schweitzer, Albert. *The Mysticism of Paul the Apostle.* London: Black, 1931.

Smedes, Lewis B. *Union with Christ.* Grand Rapids: Eerdmans, 1983.

Stein, Robert. "Baptism in Luke-Acts." In *Believer's Baptism,* ed. Thomas R. Schreiner and Shawn D. Wright, 35-66. Nashville: B&H Academic, 2006.

Stewart, James S. *A Man in Christ.* Vancouver: Regent College Publishing, 1935.

VanDrunen, David. *BioEthics and the Christian Life.* Wheaton, IL: Crossway, 2009.

Vos, Geerhardus. *The Pauline Eschatology.* Phillipsburg, NJ: P&R Publishing, 1994.

Walton, John H. *Ancient Near Eastern Thought and the Old Testament.* Grand Rapids: Baker Academic, 2006.

Witherington, III, Ben. *Paul's Narrative Thought World*. Louisville: Westminster John Knox, 1994.

Wright, Christopher J.H. *The Mission of God*. Downers Grove, IL: IVP Academic, 2006.

Wright, N.T. *The Climax of the Covenant*. Minneapolis: Fortress Press, 1993.

_____. *The Resurrection of the Son of God*. Minneapolis: Fortress, 2003.

Made in the USA
Charleston, SC
26 January 2012